BIBLE STORIES
COLORING BOOK FOR KIDS

This book belongs to:

Christian
Faith

Bible Stories Coloring Book for Kids:
Christian Coloring Book for Children with Biblical Illustrations
of the Most Memorable Scenes from the Old Testament

ISBN-13 : 979-8849444390

Test Color Page

Fall in Garden

Genesis 3:1-19

In the beginning, God created a beautiful garden called Eden, where He put the first man and woman, Adam and Eve. God gave them everything they needed to be happy and healthy. He also gave them one rule: they could eat from any tree in the garden, except for the tree of the knowledge of good and evil. God warned them that if they ate from that tree, they would die.

One day, a sneaky serpent came to Eve and asked her, "Did God really say you must not eat from any tree in the garden?" Eve replied, "We may eat from the trees in the garden, but God said we must not eat from the tree in the middle of the garden or touch it, or we will die." The serpent lied to Eve, saying, "You will not surely die. God knows that when you eat from it, your eyes will be opened, and you will be like God, knowing good and evil."

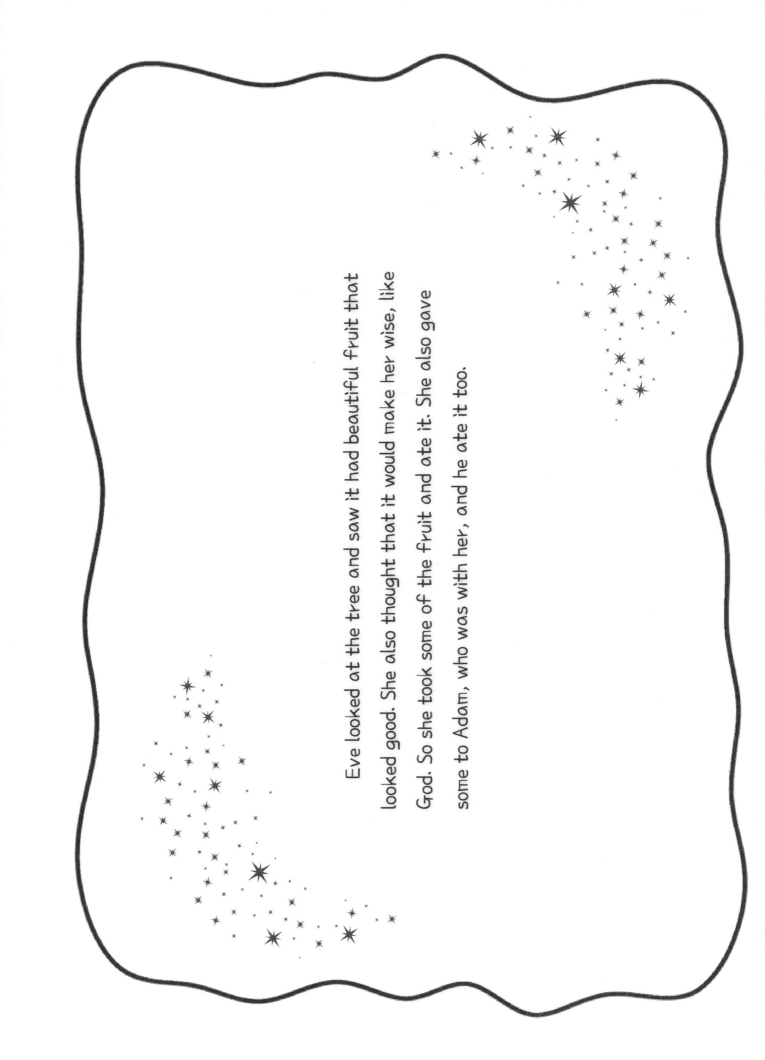

Eve looked at the tree and saw it had beautiful fruit that looked good. She also thought that it would make her wise, like God. So she took some of the fruit and ate it. She also gave some to Adam, who was with her, and he ate it too.

As soon as they ate the fruit, they realized they were naked and felt ashamed. They quickly sewed some fig leaves together and made clothes for themselves.

Then they heard God walking in the garden in the cool of the day. They were afraid and hid from Him among the trees. But God called to Adam and said, "Where are you?" Adam answered, "I heard You in the garden, and I was afraid because I was naked, so I hid."

God asked, "Who told you that you were naked? Have you eaten from the tree that I commanded you not to eat from?" Adam blamed Eve and said, "The woman You gave me, she gave me some fruit from the tree, and I ate it." God then asked Eve, "What have you done?" Eve blamed the serpent and said, "The serpent deceived me, and I ate."

God was very angry with the serpent, the woman, and the man. He cursed the serpent and said, "You will crawl on your belly and eat dust all the days of your life. And I will make you and the woman enemies, and your children and her children enemies. Her child will crush your head, and you will strike his heel." This was a prophecy about Jesus, who would come from Eve's descendants and defeat the evil one behind the serpent.

God also punished the woman and said, "I will make your pains in childbirth very severe. You will have a strong desire for your husband, but he will rule over you." God also punished the man and said, "Because you listened to your wife and ate from the tree, the ground is cursed because of you. You will have to work hard and sweat to grow food from it. It will produce thorns and thistles for you, and you will eat the plants of the field. You will work until you die and return to the dust since you were made from it."

God then made clothes of animal skins for Adam and Eve and clothed them. He also drove them out of the Garden of Eden and placed cherubim, or angels, and a flaming sword to guard the way to the Tree of Life. He did this to prevent them from eating from the Tree of Life and living forever in their sinful state.

This is how sin entered the world and separated us from God. But God still loved us and had a plan to save us. He sent His Son, Jesus Christ, to die on the cross for our sins and rise again from the dead. Whoever believes in Him will not perish but have eternal life.

Abram in Egypt

Genesis 12:10—20

After a long time, since Adam and Eve were cast out of heaven, there was a man named Abram who loved God very much. He had a beautiful wife named Sarai, and they traveled together to a land that God had promised to give them. But when they got there, they found out there was not enough food for everyone. The land was very dry, and nothing could grow. This is called a famine.

Abram was worried about his family, so he decided to go to another country called Egypt, where there was plenty of food and water. He packed up his tents, his animals, and his servants, and he set off with Sarai.

But as they were getting closer to Egypt, he had a problem. He realized that Sarai was so beautiful that the Egyptians would want to take her away from him. They might even harm him to get her.

So, he came up with a plan. He said to Sarai, "Listen, my dear, I know that you are a very beautiful woman. When the Egyptians see you, they will say, 'This is his wife.' And they will harm me, but they will let you live. So please, say that you are my sister, not my wife. That way, they will treat me well for your sake, and they will not harm me."

Sarai agreed to do what Abram asked, even though she was scared. She loved her husband and wanted to protect him. But she also trusted God to take care of them.

When they arrived in Egypt, everything happened just as Abram had said.

The Egyptians saw that Sarai was very beautiful, and they told the king of Egypt, who was called Pharaoh. Pharaoh wanted to have Sarai as his wife, so he took her into his palace. He also gave Abram many gifts, such as sheep, cattle, donkeys, camels, and servants. He thought that Abram was Sarai's brother, and he wanted to make him happy.

But God was not happy with what Pharaoh had done. He knew that Sarai was Abram's wife and that Pharaoh had taken her away from him. God loved Abram and Sarai, and He wanted them to be together. So, He sent a terrible sickness to Pharaoh and his household. They all became very ill, and they suffered a lot.

Pharaoh soon found out that it was because of Sarai. He called Abram and said, "What have you done to me? Why didn't you tell me that she was your wife? Why did you say, 'She is my sister,' so that I took her to be my wife? Now then, here is your wife. Take her and go!"

Pharaoh was very angry with Abram, and he ordered his men to send him away, along with Sarai and everything he had. He did not want to keep them in his land anymore because he was afraid of God's punishment.

Abram and Sarai left Egypt and went back to the land that God had promised them. They were very happy to be together again, and they thanked God for saving them from Pharaoh. They learned to trust God more and to be honest with each other. God blessed them and made them a great nation.

Jacob's Ladder

Genesis 28:10-22

There was a young man named Jacob, Abraham's grandson, who had to run away from his home. He had tricked his father, Isaac, into giving him a special blessing that belonged to his older brother, Esau. Esau was very angry with Jacob and wanted to harm him. So Jacob's mother, Rebekah, told him to go to her brother Laban's house in a faraway land called Haran. She hoped that Esau would calm down and forgive Jacob someday.

Jacob packed his things and left his home. He walked for many days and nights until he came to a place where he decided to rest.

He found a large stone and used it as a pillow. He lay down on the ground and fell asleep.

As he slept, he had a wonderful dream. He saw a ladder that reached from the earth to the heaven. And on the ladder, he saw angels going up and down. They carried messages from God to the people and from the people to God. And above the ladder, he saw God himself, shining with glory and love.

God spoke to Jacob and said, "I am the Lord, the God of your grandfather Abraham and your father Isaac. I will give you and your descendants the land where you are lying. Your descendants will be as many as the dust of the earth, and they will spread in all directions. Through you and your descendants, all the families of the earth will be blessed. I am with you, and I will protect you wherever you go. I will bring you back to this land. I will not leave you until I have done everything I have promised you."

Jacob woke up from his dream and was amazed. He said, "Surely the Lord is in this place, and I did not know it. This is a holy place. This is the house of God and the gate of heaven."

He got up and took the stone that he had used as a pillow. He set it up as a monument and poured oil on it. He named the place Bethel, which means "house of God." He made a vow to God and said, "If God will be with me and protect me on this journey, and give me food and clothes, and bring me back safely to my father's house, then the Lord will be my God. And this stone that I have set up as a monument will be God's house. And I will give God a tenth of everything He gives me."

Then Jacob continued his journey to Haran, where he met his uncle Laban and his cousins Rachel and Leah. He worked for Laban for many years and married Rachel and Leah. He had twelve sons and one daughter, who became the ancestors of the twelve tribes of Israel. God blessed Jacob and his family and kept his promise to bring him back to the land of his father. Jacob never forgot his dream at Bethel, and he always worshiped God as his Lord.

God Speaks to Moses

Exodus 3:1–12

There was a man named Moses who had a very special job. He was

a shepherd, which means he took care of sheep. He loved his sheep and

made sure they had enough food and water. He also protected them

from wild animals and thieves.

One day, Moses led his sheep to a place where they could find some grass and water. He came to a mountain called Horeb, also known as the mountain of God. He did not know why it was called that, but he thought it was a good place for his sheep.

As he was walking, he saw something extraordinary. He saw a bush that was on fire but did not burn up. The fire kept burning, but the bush stayed green and alive. Moses was curious and wanted to see what was going on. He said, "I will go over and see this amazing thing. Why does the bush not burn up?"

But as he got closer, he heard a voice coming from the bush. The voice said, "Moses, Moses!" And Moses said, "Here I am." The voice said, "Do not come any closer. Take off your sandals, for the place where you are standing is holy ground."

Moses was surprised and scared. He wondered who was talking to him from the bush. He took off his sandals and hid his face because he was afraid to look at the fire.

Then the voice said, "I am the God of your father, the God of Abraham, the God of Isaac, and the God of Jacob." Moses knew that these were the names of his ancestors, who had worshiped God long ago. He realized this was the same God who had made the world and everything in it.

God said to Moses, "I have seen the suffering of My people in Egypt. I have heard their cries, and I care about them. I have come to rescue them from the cruel king of Egypt, who makes them work as slaves. I have come to bring them to a new land, a land that is good and beautiful, a land that is full of milk and honey. This is the land where the Canaanites, the Hittites, the Amorites, the Perizzites, the Hivites, and the Jebusites live. But I will give it to My people as their own home."

God told Moses, "I have chosen you to be my messenger. I want you to go to the king of Egypt and tell him to let My people go. I want you to lead My people out of Egypt and bring them to the land that I have promised them."

But Moses was afraid and said to God, "Who am I that I should go to Pharaoh and bring the Israelites out of Egypt?" God said to Moses, "I will be with you. I will help you and guide you. I will show you a sign that I have sent you. When you have brought the people out of Egypt, you will worship Me on this mountain."

Moses told God, "But what if the people do not believe me? What if they ask me, 'What is the name of the God who sent you?' What shall I tell them?" God said to Moses, "I am who I am. This is what you are to say to the Israelites: 'I am has sent me to you.' Tell them, 'The Lord, the God of your fathers, the God of Abraham, the God of Isaac, and the God of Jacob, has sent me to you.'"

God told Moses, "Go and gather the elders of the people and tell them what I have said to you. Tell them that I have seen their misery and that I have come to save them. Tell them I will bring them to the land I promised them. They will listen to you and follow you. Then you and the elders will go to the king of Egypt and say to him, 'The Lord, the God of the Hebrews, has met with us. Please let us go three days' journey into the wilderness, so that we may worship our God.'"

"But I know that the king of Egypt will not let you go unless I force him. So, I will do many wonders and miracles in Egypt to show him My power and glory. I will strike Egypt with plagues and disasters until he lets you go. And I will make the Egyptians favor you and give you many gifts, such as silver, gold, and clothes. You will not leave Egypt empty-handed. You will leave with great wealth and honor."

"But before you go, I will give you some signs to prove that I have sent you. Take your shepherd's staff with you, and I will show you what to do with it." Then He said to Moses, "Throw your staff on the ground." Moses did as God told him, and his staff turned into a snake. Moses was afraid and ran away from it. God told Moses, "Reach out your hand and take it by the tail." Moses did as God told him, and the snake turned back into a staff. God told Moses, "This is so that they may believe that the Lord, the God of their fathers, the God of Abraham, the God of Isaac, and the God of Jacob, has appeared to you."

God told Moses, "Now put your hand inside your cloak." Moses did as God told him, and when he took it out, his hand was leprous, white as snow. God said to Moses, "Put it back into your cloak." Moses did as God told him, and when he took it out again, it was restored, like the rest of his flesh. God told Moses, "If they do not believe you or pay attention to the first sign, they may believe the second one." He continues, "But if they do not believe either of these signs or listen to you, take some water from the Nile and pour it on the dry ground. The water you take from the river will become blood on the ground."

"These are the signs that I have given you to show the people that I have sent you. But I know that you are not good at speaking. You are slow and hesitant with words."

Moses said to God, "Please, Lord, send someone else. I am not eloquent, either in the past or since You have spoken to Your servant. I am slow of speech and tongue."

God said to Moses, "Who gave human beings their mouths? Who makes them deaf or mute? Who gives them sight or makes them blind? Is it not I, the Lord? Now go; I will help you speak and teach you what to say."

But Moses still said to God, "Please, Lord, send someone else." Then God became angry with Moses and said, "What about your brother, Aaron the Levite? I know he can speak well. He is already on his way to meet you and will be glad to see you. You shall speak to him and put words in his mouth; I will help both of you speak and teach you what to do. He will speak to the people for you, and it will be as if he were your mouth and as if you were God to him. But take this staff in your hand so you can perform the signs with it."

Moses listened to God and trusted Him. He left the burning bush and went back to his sheep. He prepared to go to Egypt and do what God had told him to do. On the way, he met his brother Aaron and told him everything God had said. He also showed him the signs that God had given him. Aaron agreed to help Moses and to speak for him. They trusted God and hoped that God would keep his promise. They did not know what would happen but knew God was with them.

The Israelites Cross the Red Sea

Exodus 14:5-31

Pharaoh was very stubborn and cruel and did not want to let the Israelites go. He made them work harder, ignoring the signs and wonders that God did through Moses and Aaron.

But God had a plan to save His people. He sent ten terrible plagues to Egypt, one after another, to show his power and judgment. He turned the water of the Nile into blood. He sent frogs, gnats, flies, livestock diseases, boils, hail, locusts, darkness. Pharaoh promised to let the Israelites go each time, but then he changed his mind and refused. He hardened his heart and did not listen to God. But God protected His people from the plagues. He distinguished between the Egyptians and the Israelites so the plagues did not harm them.

Finally, after the tenth plague, Pharaoh let the Israelites go. He was afraid of God. He told Moses and Aaron to take their people and animals and leave Egypt. The Israelites left Egypt with great wealth and honor. They had been slaves for 430 years, but now they were free. Moses led the people out of Egypt, following God's guidance. He brought them to the edge of the Red Sea, where they camped by the water.

But Pharaoh changed his mind again. He regretted letting the Israelites go, and he wanted to get them back. He said to himself, "What have I done? I have lost my slaves and my workers!" He gathered his army and his chariots, and he chased after the Israelites. He wanted to catch them and bring them back to Egypt.

The Israelites saw the Egyptians coming after them, and they were terrified. They cried out to God and to Moses. They said, "Why did you bring us out of Egypt to die in the wilderness? Was it because there were no graves in Egypt? We told you to leave us alone and let us serve the Egyptians. It would have been better for us to be slaves than to die here."

But Moses said to them, "Do not be afraid. Stand still and see the salvation of the Lord. He will fight for you, and you will see the Egyptians no more. The Lord will show you His power and His glory today."

Then God asked Moses, "Why are you crying out to me? Tell the people to move forward. Raise your staff and stretch your hand over the sea, and I will divide the water. The people will go through the sea on dry ground. I will harden the hearts of the Egyptians, and they will follow them. I will show them who I am and get honor over Pharaoh and his army."

Then God moved the pillar of cloud and fire from before the Israelites to behind them. He made a wall of darkness between them and the Egyptians so they could not see each other. Then Moses stretched his hand over the sea, and God sent a strong wind to blow the water apart. He made a path through the sea, with walls of water on both sides.

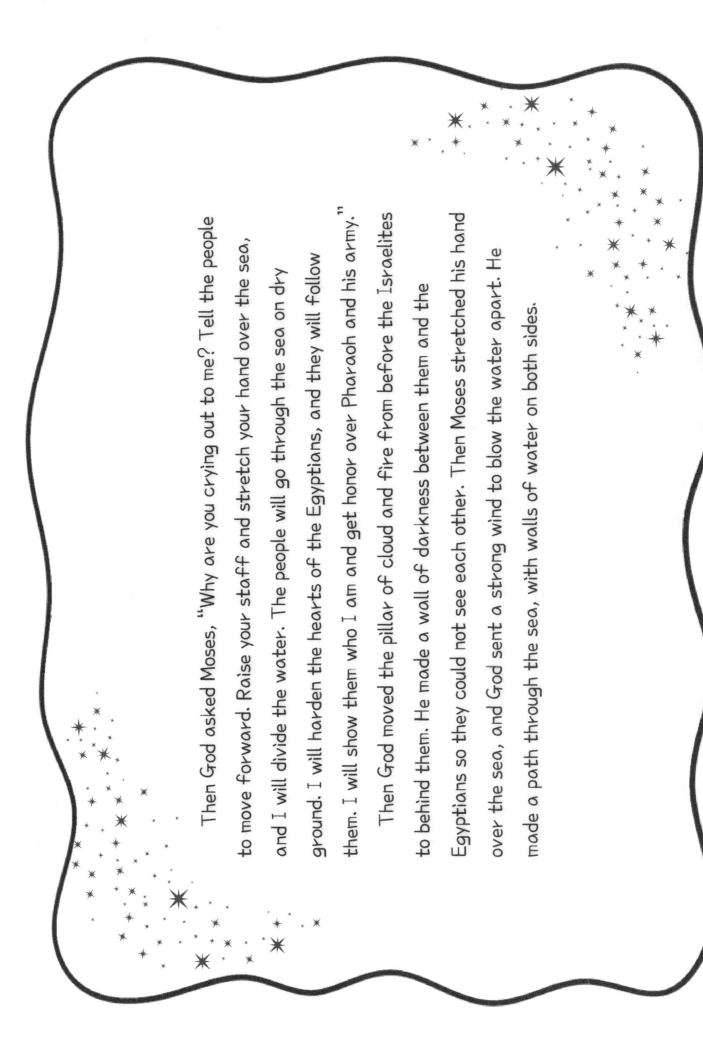

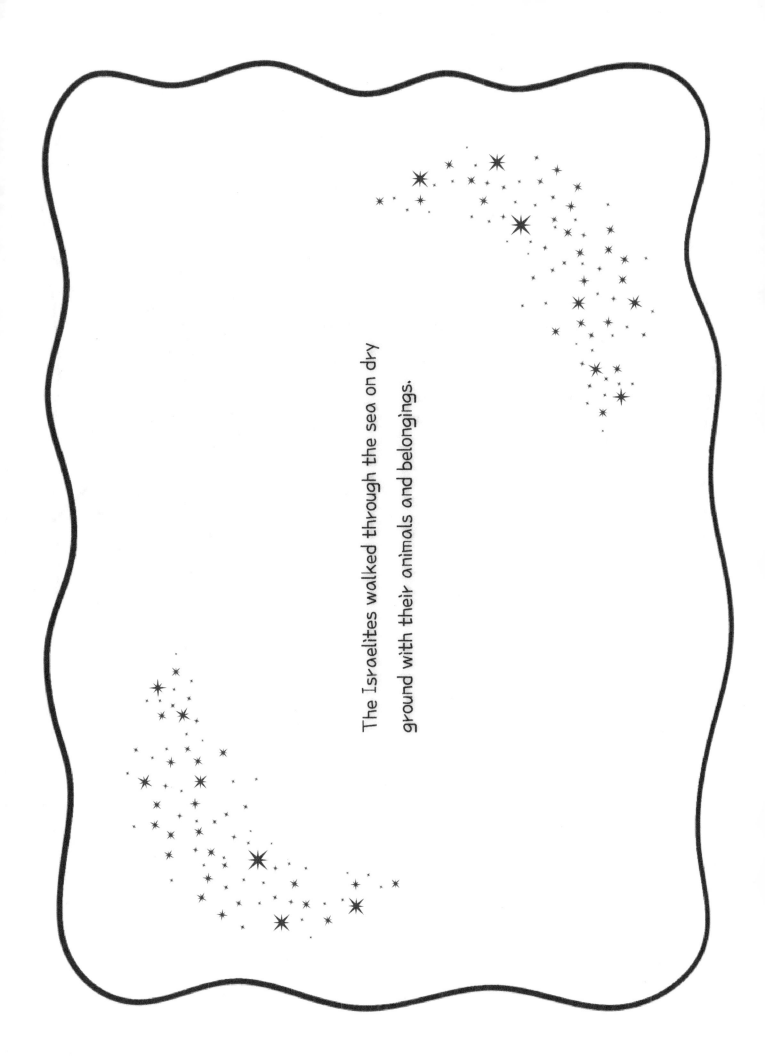

The Israelites walked through the sea on dry ground with their animals and belongings.

The Egyptians followed them into the sea with their horses and their chariots. But God made their wheels get stuck, and their chariots break down.

They realized that God was fighting against them, and they tried to turn back. But it was too late.

God told Moses, "Stretch out your hand over the sea again, and the water will return." Moses did as God told him, and the water came crashing down on the Egyptians. They were all drowned in the sea.

The Israelites saw what God had done, and they were amazed. They feared God and trusted Him. They also praised Him and worshiped Him. They sang a song of victory and joy, thanking God for saving them from their enemies. They said, "The Lord is my strength and my song; He has become my salvation. He is my God, and I will praise Him; He is my father's God, and I will exalt Him. The Lord is a warrior; the Lord is His name. He has thrown the horse and its rider into the sea. He has triumphed gloriously."

The Israelites continued their journey to the land that God had promised them. They faced many challenges and difficulties, but God was with them. He guided, protected, provided for, and taught them. He made a covenant with them and gave them His law. He also gave them His presence and His glory. He was their God, and they were His people.

The Lord Gives Water

from a Rock

Exodus 17:1–7

The Israelites were on their way to a wonderful land that God had promised to give them. But the journey was long and hard, and sometimes they had to go through dry and barren places. One day, they came to a place called Rephidim, where they set up their tents. But there was a big problem: there was no water for them to drink!

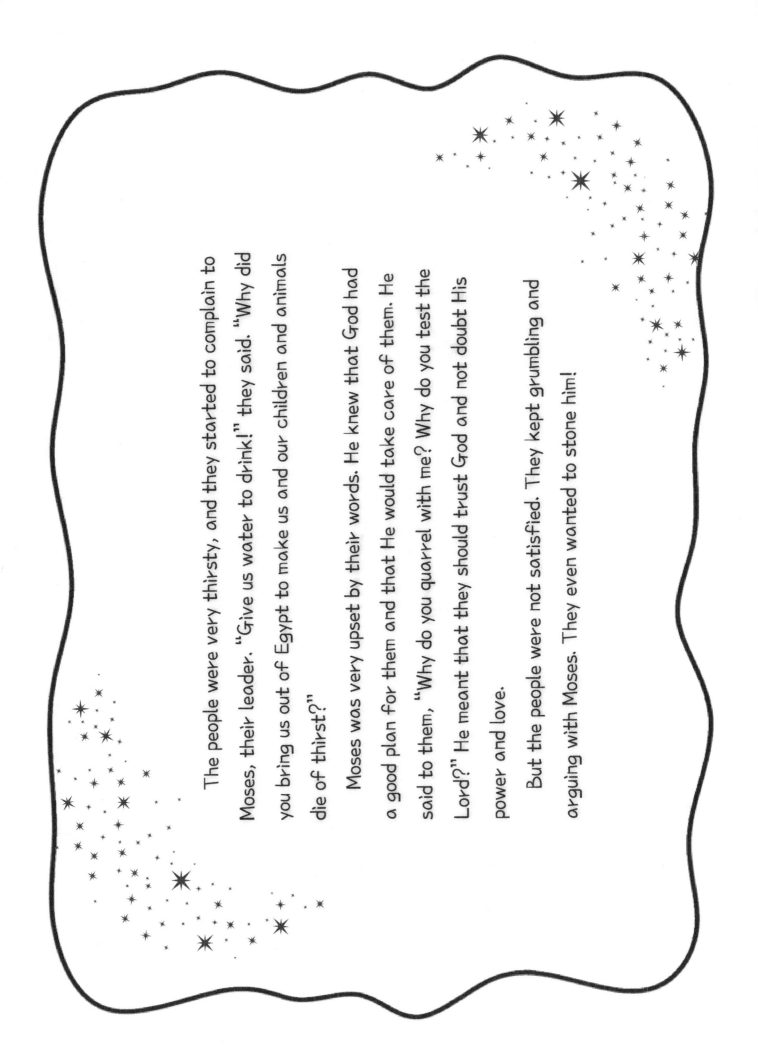

The people were very thirsty, and they started to complain to Moses, their leader. "Give us water to drink!" they said. "Why did you bring us out of Egypt to make us and our children and animals die of thirst?"

Moses was very upset by their words. He knew that God had a good plan for them and that He would take care of them. He said to them, "Why do you quarrel with me? Why do you test the Lord?" He meant that they should trust God and not doubt His power and love.

But the people were not satisfied. They kept grumbling and arguing with Moses. They even wanted to stone him!

Moses was afraid, and he cried out to the Lord, "What shall I do with these people? They are almost ready to stone me!"

The Lord heard Moses' prayer, and He answered him. He said, "Go out in front of the people. Take some of the elders of Israel with you, and take the staff that you used to strike the Nile River. I will stand before you on the rock at Horeb. Strike the rock, and water will come out of it for the people to drink."

Moses did as the Lord told him. He took some of the elders and his staff, and he went to the rock. He saw the Lord standing there, and he struck the rock with his staff. To his amazement, water gushed out of the rock! It was enough for all the people and their animals to drink. The people were happy and grateful, and they praised God for His miracle.

Moses called the place Massah and Meribah, which means testing and quarreling. He wanted to remind the people that they had tested the Lord and quarreled with Him. He also wanted them to remember that God was always with them and that He would provide for their needs.

Elisha Helps a Poor Widow

2 Kings 4:1—7

About 800 years before Jesus was born, in a land called Israel there was a prophet named Elisha. A prophet is someone who speaks God's words to the people. Israel was God's special nation, but many of the people and kings did not obey God or worship Him. They followed false gods and idols and did many evil things. God was not happy with them, and He sent prophets like Elisha to warn them and to show them His power and love.

Elisha was a faithful servant of God, and he did many amazing miracles with God's help. A miracle is something that is impossible for humans to do but possible for God to do. Elisha could make sick people well, multiply food, raise the dead, and even make an iron axe head float on water! He did these miracles to help people who trusted God and to show God's glory and kindness.

One day, a woman came to Elisha with a big problem. She was the wife of one of the other prophets, who had died. She was very poor, and she had no money to pay her debts. The person she owed money to was very cruel, and he wanted to take her two sons as slaves in place of debt. The woman was very sad and afraid, and she cried out to Elisha for help.

Elisha asked her, "What can I do for you? What do you have in your house?" The woman said, "I have nothing at all, except a small jar of olive oil." Olive oil was used for cooking, lighting lamps, and anointing people. Elisha told her, "Go and borrow as many empty jars as you can from your neighbors. Then go inside your house, shut the door, and pour oil from your jar into all the other jars. Set aside the full ones."

The woman did as Elisha said. She went to her neighbors and asked them for empty jars. They gave her many jars of different shapes and sizes. She brought them all to her house, and closed the door with her sons. She took her small jar of oil, and started to pour it into the other jars. To her surprise, the oil kept flowing and flowing and flowing, filling up one jar after another. She asked her sons to bring her more jars, but they said, "There are no more jars left." Then the oil stopped flowing.

The woman was amazed and happy. She had so much oil now that she could sell it and pay her debts.

She ran to Elisha and told him what happened. Elisha said, "Go, sell the oil, and pay your debt. You and your sons can live on the rest."

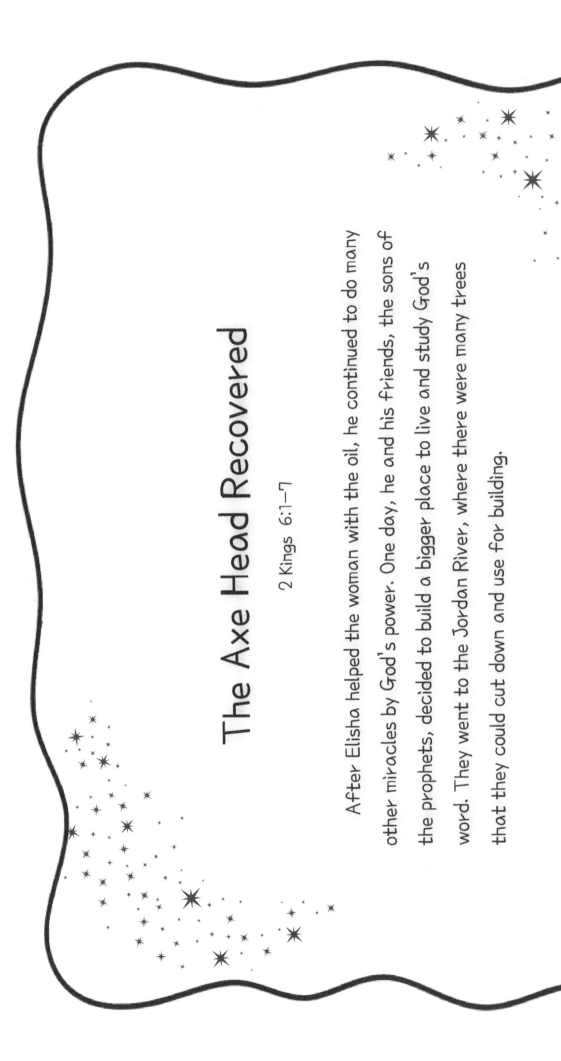

The Axe Head Recovered

2 Kings 6:1-7

After Elisha helped the woman with the oil, he continued to do many other miracles by God's power. One day, he and his friends, the sons of the prophets, decided to build a bigger place to live and study God's word. They went to the Jordan River, where there were many trees that they could cut down and use for building.

They worked hard, chopping down the trees and carrying the beams. They were having fun, singing songs and telling stories. Elisha was with them, encouraging them and teaching them. They felt happy and blessed to be with the man of God.

But then, something bad happened. One of the sons of the prophets was cutting down a tree when his axe head fell into the water. He was very upset because the axe was not his own but borrowed from someone else. He knew that he had to return it or pay for it. But how could he find it in the deep water?

He cried out to Elisha, "Oh no, master! The axe head is gone, and it was borrowed!" Elisha heard him and came to see what was wrong. He asked him, "Where did it fall?" The man pointed to the spot where the axe head had sunk. Elisha looked at the water and prayed to God.

Then he did something amazing. He took a stick and threw it into the water, right where the axe head had fallen. As soon as the stick touched the water, the iron axe head floated up to the surface like a cork. The man could not believe his eyes. He was so happy and relieved. He thanked Elisha and God for the miracle.

Elisha said to him, "Pick it up for yourself." The man reached out his hand and took the axe head. He put it back on the handle and continued to work with his friends. They all praised God for His goodness and power. They learned that God cared about them, even in the small things. They also learned to be careful with what they borrowed and to be honest and responsible.

The Two Paths

Psalm 1:1–6

Happy is the one who walks not in evil ways,

Who stands not with the sinners or the mockers sways.

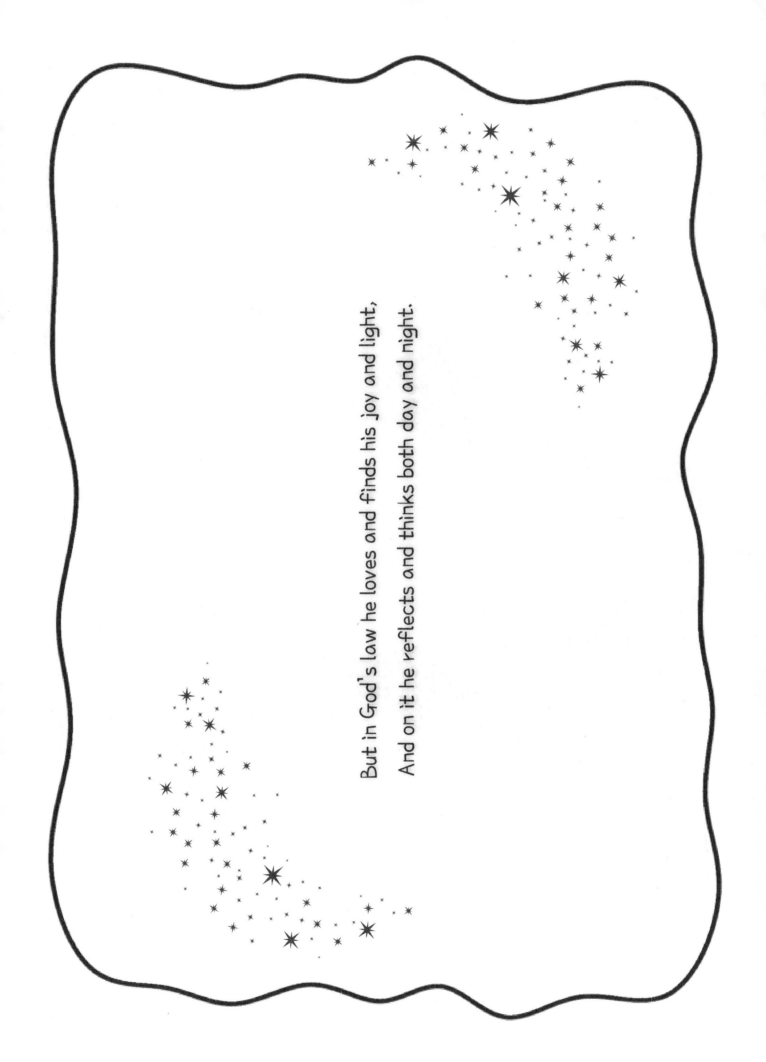

But in God's law he loves and finds his joy and light,
And on it he reflects and thinks both day and night.

He is like a tree that by the water stands,

Its roots are firm and deep, its leaves are green and grand.

He trusts in God's and follows His commands,

He spreads His love and peace to every heart and land.

It bears its fruit in season, and it does not wither,

Whatever he may do, the Lord will make it glitter.

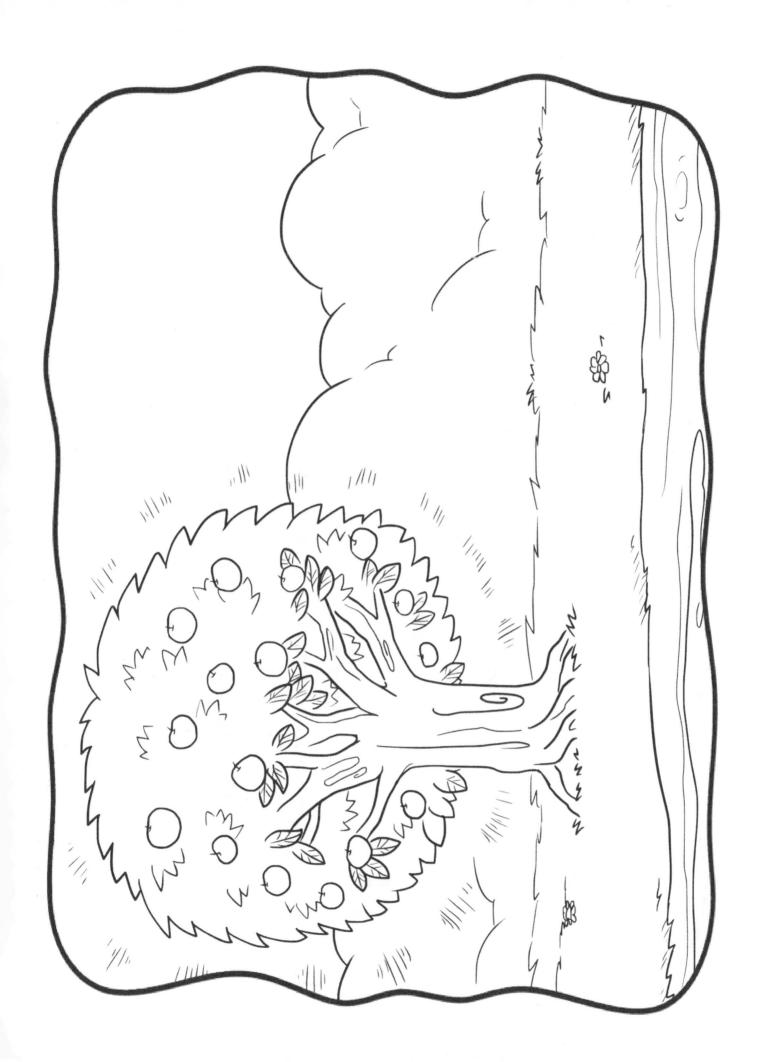

But not so are the wicked, they are like the dust,

That the wind scatters far, and no one knows or trusts.

They have no place or portion in God's holy sight,

They will not stand or last in the day of judgment's might.

For God watches the righteous, and He guides their way,

He knows their thoughts and deeds, and He listens to their say.

But the wicked's way is lost, and it leads to woe,

They will perish in their guilt, and they will face their foe.

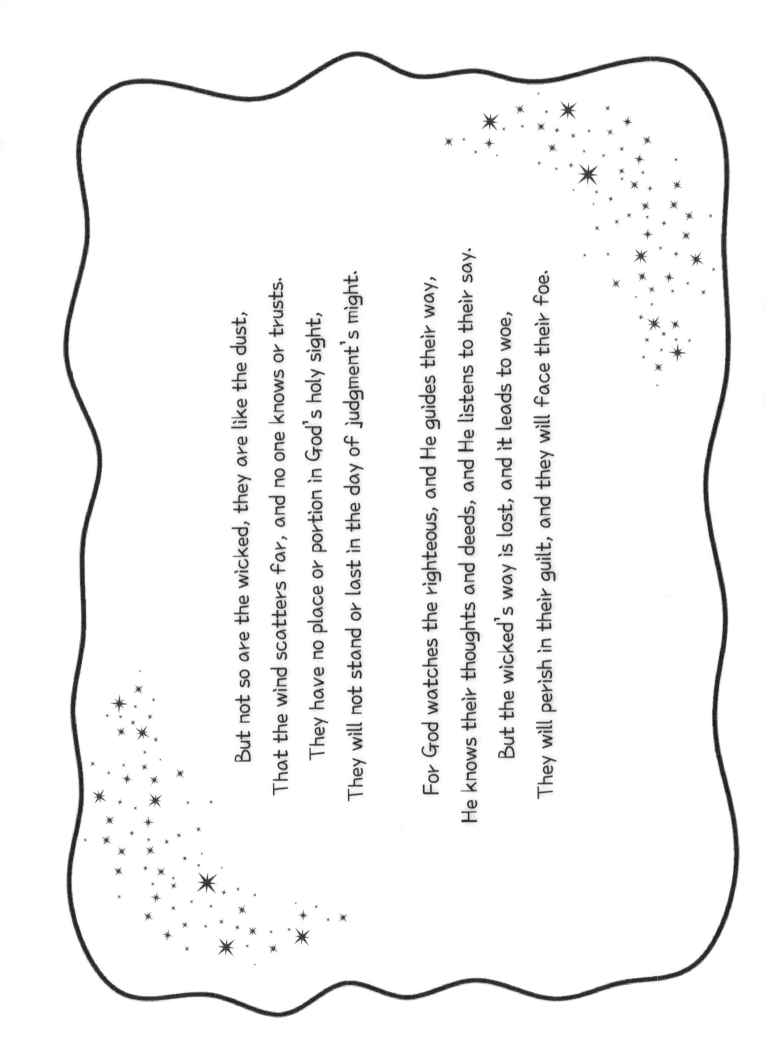

The Lord Is My Shepherd

Psalm 23:1–6

My Lord is my shepherd, He cares for me,

He leads me to green fields, where I can rest in harmony.

He guides me to calm waters, where I can drink and be refreshed,

He restores my soul, He shows me the way of righteousness.

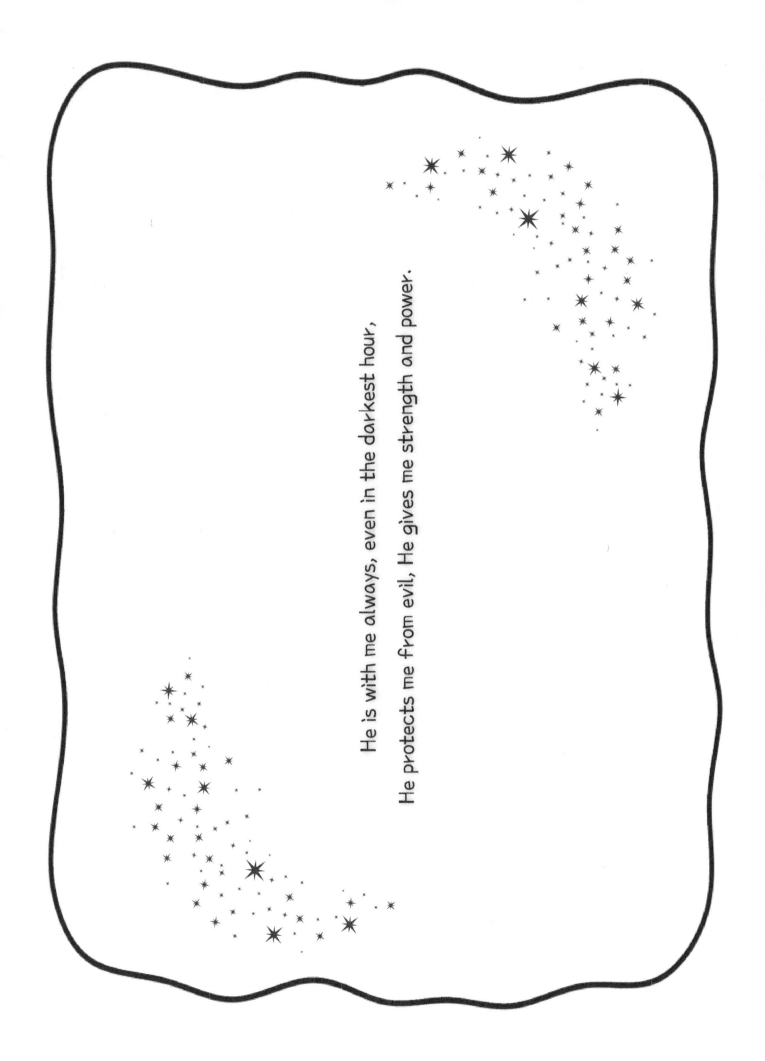

He is with me always, even in the darkest hour,
He protects me from evil, He gives me strength and power.

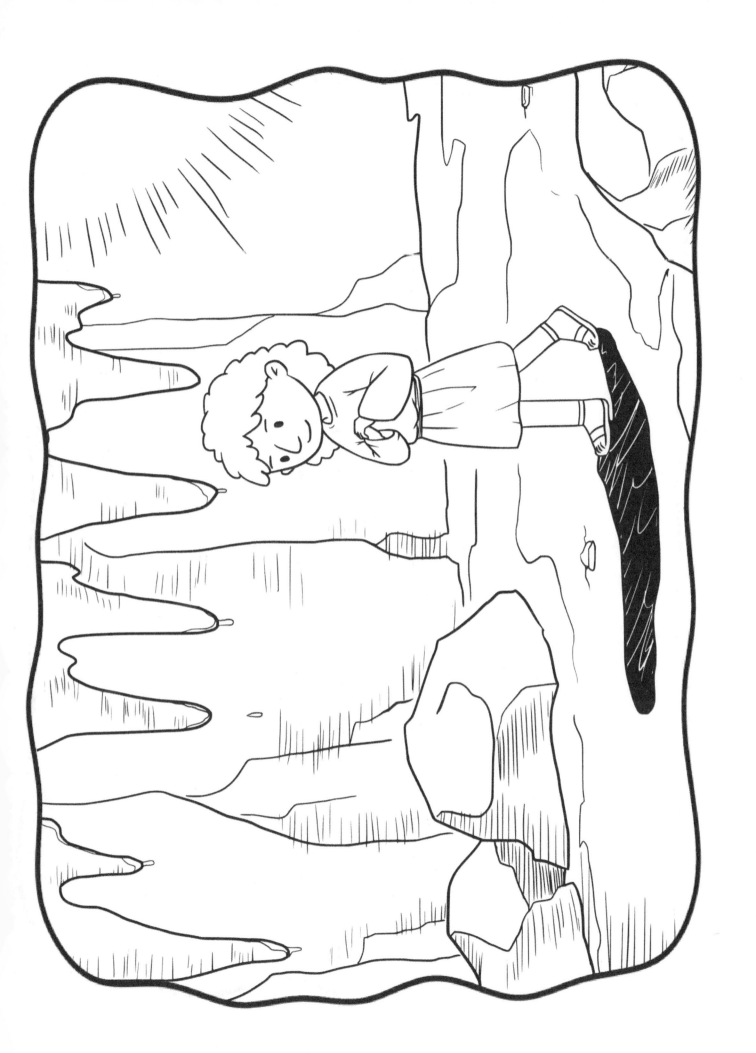

He comforts me with His rod and staff, He is my faithful friend,

He prepares a feast for me, He blesses me without end.

He fills my cup with joy, He anoints my head with oil,

He showers me with grace, He rewards me for my toil.

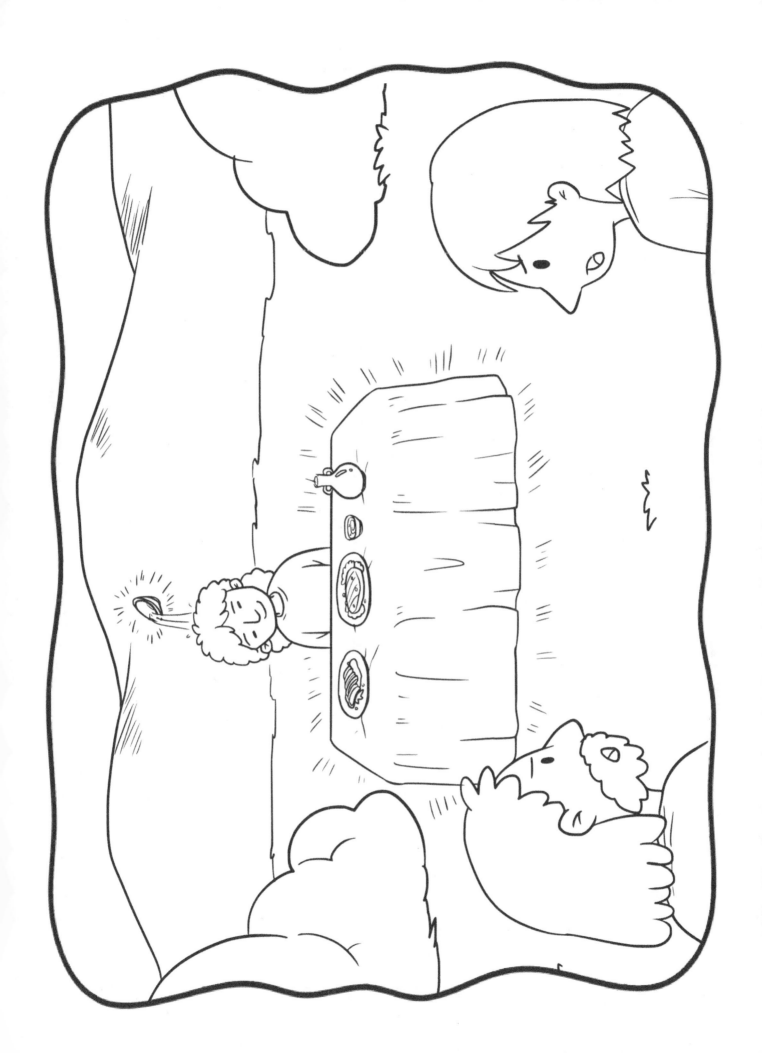

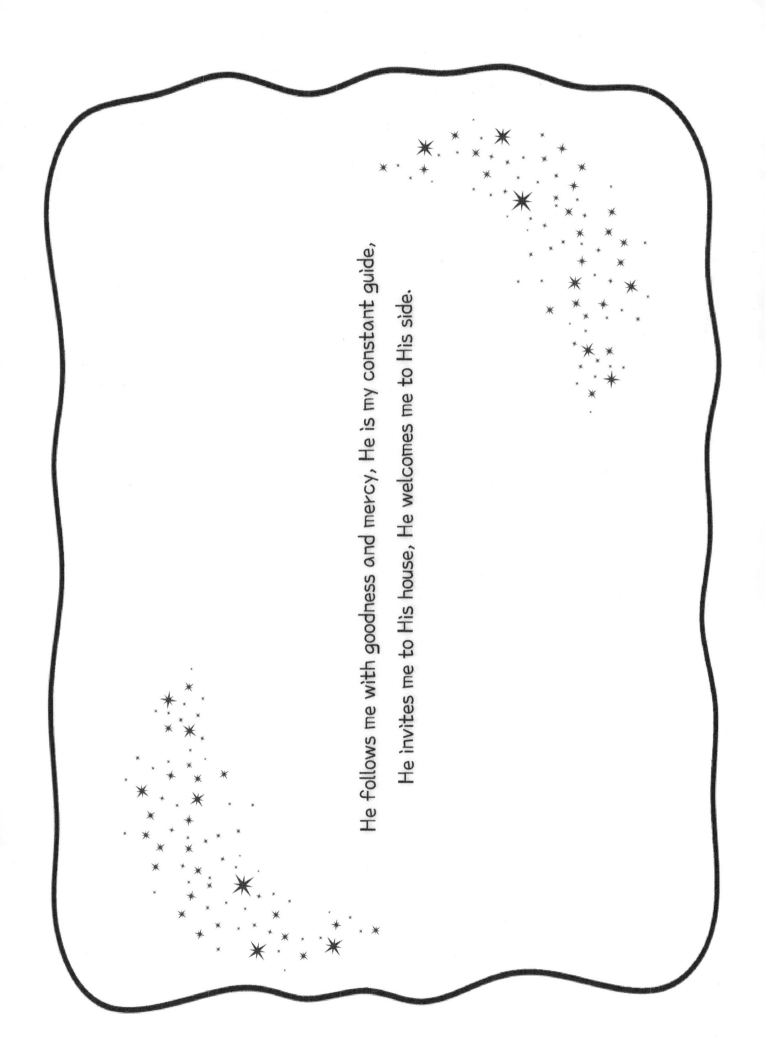

He follows me with goodness and mercy, He is my constant guide,

He invites me to His house, He welcomes me to His side.

Jonah Runs

Jonah 1:1–16; 2:1–11

There was a man named Jonah who was a prophet of God. God told Jonah to go to a city called Nineveh and tell the people there to stop doing bad things and turn back to God. But Jonah did not want to go to Nineveh, so he decided to run away from God and go to another place.

He went to a port called Joppa and found a boat that was going to Tarshish, which was very far away from Nineveh. He paid the fare and got on the boat, hoping to escape from God. But he did not know that God sees everything and knows everything and that no one can hide from Him.

As the boat sailed on the sea, God sent a great storm that made the waves crash and the wind howl. The boat was in danger of breaking apart, and the sailors were very afraid. They prayed to their gods, but nothing happened. They also threw some of the cargo into the sea to make the ship lighter. But the storm did not stop.

Meanwhile, Jonah was sleeping in the lower part of the ship. He did not care about the storm or the sailors. He was too tired from running away from God. The boat captain approached him and asked, "How can you sleep? Get up and call on your God! Maybe He will help us, and we will not die."

The sailors also came to Jonah and said, "Let us cast lots to find out who is causing this trouble." Casting lots was a way of finding out God's will by using sticks or stones or other things. They cast lots, and the lot fell on Jonah. They asked him, "Who are you? Where do you come from? What do you do? Why is this happening to us?"

Jonah told them, "I am a Hebrew, and I worship the Lord, the God of heaven and earth, who made the sea and the land. I am running away from Him because He told me to go to Nineveh, and I did not want to go."

The sailors were shocked and scared. They knew that the Lord was a mighty God and that He was angry with Jonah. They asked him, "What should we do to you to make the sea calm down?"

Jonah said, "Pick me up and throw me into the sea, and it will become calm. I know this is my fault and have brought this storm upon you."

The sailors did not want to do this because they did not want to harm Jonah. They tried to row back to the land, but they could not. The storm was too strong. They cried out to the Lord, "Please, Lord, do not let us die for taking this man's life. Do not hold us guilty for harming an innocent man, for you, Lord, have done as you pleased."

Then they took Jonah and threw him into the sea. And the sea became calm. The sailors were amazed, and they praised the Lord. They also made promises to Him to serve Him and obey Him.

But what happened to Jonah? Did he drown in the sea? No, he did not. God had a plan for him. God sent a big fish, a whale, to swallow Jonah. And Jonah was in the belly of the fish for three days and three nights.

You might think that Jonah was dead, but Jonah was alive. He realized that God had saved him from the storm and from death. He also admitted that he had disobeyed God and done wrong. He prayed to God from inside the fish, and the Lord heard Jonah's prayer, and He was pleased with him. He spoke to the fish, and the fish vomited Jonah out onto the dry land.

And that is the end of the story of Jonah and the big fish. But it is not the end of Jonah's story. God had more to say to him, and more to teach him.

The moral of this story is that we should always listen to God and do what He tells us to do. He is everywhere, and He knows everything. He loves us, and He wants us to love Him and to love others. He also wants us to repent, which means to say sorry to Him and to change our ways when we do something wrong. He is ready to forgive us, and to help us, and to save us. He is a good God, and He deserves our praise.

The End!

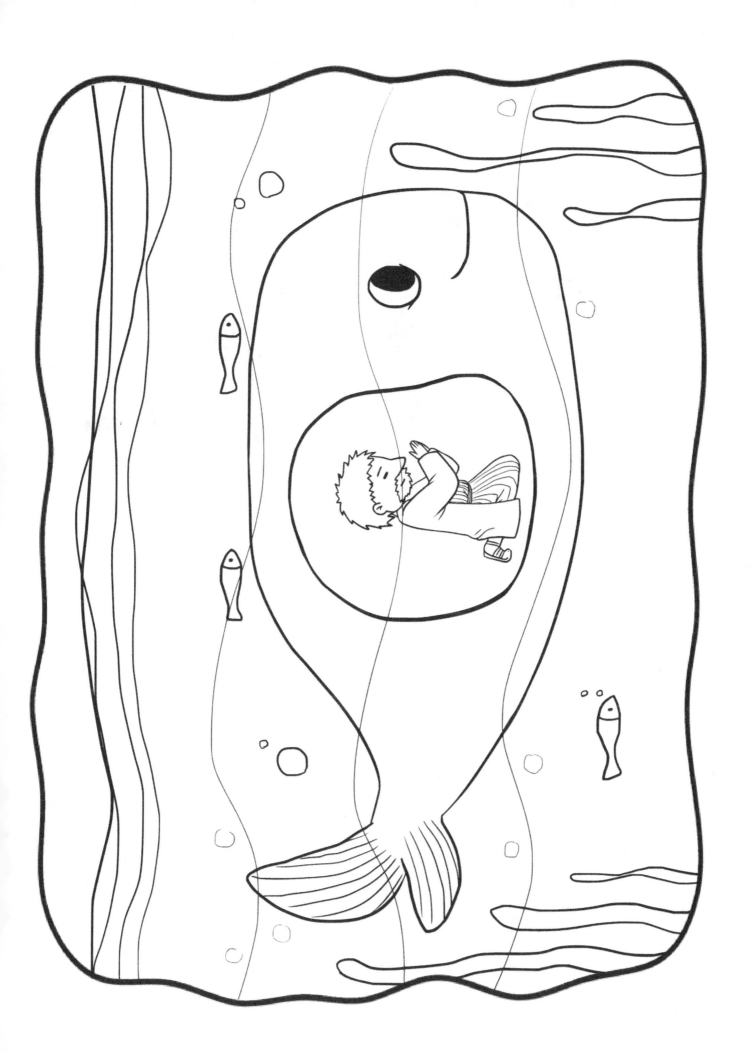

If you enjoyed our book, please consider taking a look at the New Testament version for more coloring illustrations and stories about our Lord Jesus Christ:

Link Here

Jesus as boy
Luke 2:40-52

Every year, Jesus and His parents went to a big city called Jerusalem to celebrate a festival called Passover. Passover was a time to remember how God saved His people from slavery in Egypt. They ate special bread and sang songs of praise to God.

Jesus went with His parents to Jerusalem as usual when He was twelve years old. They had a great time at the festival and learned more about God and His laws. After the festival was over, Mary and Joseph packed their bags and started to go back home with their friends and relatives.

Jesus at the home of
Martha and Mary
Luke 10:38-42

One day, Jesus Christ and His disciples came to a town where two sisters lived. Their names were Martha and Mary. They were very happy to see Jesus and invited Him to their home. They wanted to show Him their love and hospitality.

Mary was a very curious and attentive sister. She wanted to hear what Jesus had to say. She went to the living room and sat at His feet. She listened to His words and asked Him questions. She was very interested and had a lot to learn.

Made in the USA
Las Vegas, NV
27 December 2024

15407949R00059